How to Resolve Marital Issues Without Divorce

Proficient Advice on Conquering Obstacles and Reinstating Your Marriage

More Powerful Than Ever Before

Adegboye S. Aduragbemi

INTRODUCTION

Any relationship will inevitably have conflict; however, how we handle and come to terms with these differences determines how resilient and strong our relationships are. Dissimilar viewpoints, unfulfilled expectations, and the intricacies of daily existence can give rise to disputes in the delicate dance of marriage. The purpose of the "Conflict Resolution FAQ in Marriage" is to be a source of light, advice, and understanding for married couples who are trying to resolve conflicts in a civil, compassionate, and understanding manner.

You will discover a thorough list of commonly asked concerns, intelligent responses, and valuable techniques for handling marital disputes inside the pages of this book. Every concern, due to the little arguments that arise every day, the more significant issues that put our relationships to the ultimate test, is answered with understanding counsel and professional recommendations made specifically with married couples in mind.

The book "Conflict Resolution FAQ in Marriage" provides couples with a road map for converting disagreement into a chance for personal development, increased closeness, and realistic tales and scenarios. This book offers priceless advice and resources to help you resolve conflicts with resilience and confidence, whether you're a newlywed starting your marriage journey or a seasoned couple looking to deepen your relationship.

May the experiences of others that you share, the insight of professionals, and the bravery to accept conflict as a means of building a stronger bond and understanding within your marriage provide you comfort and inspiration as you set out on this path of introspection and learning.

Together, let's explore the ageless issues, complex dynamics, and exquisite nature of marital dispute resolution.

Chapter One

Conflict management in relationship

When conflict is not adequately managed in a relationship

Emma and Mark appeared to have it all in their lovely home, lucrative careers, and picture-perfect family in the tranquil suburbs of Willowbrook. Behind closed doors, though, unspoken tensions and unfulfilled expectations were causing their relationship to implode.

The conflict was nothing new to Emma, a devoted attorney with a strong sense of justice, and Mark, a successful executive hoping to go up the corporate ladder. Their divergent approaches to dispute resolution and communication styles frequently resulted in tense exchanges and unresolved conflicts.

One fateful evening, a quarrel over funds turned into a full-blown confrontation, bringing their difficulties to a peak. Emma became enraged and accused Mark of being authoritarian and indifferent to her needs, upset by his refusal to make concessions and establish common ground. Feeling misinterpreted and assaulted, Mark reacted defensively, declining to have a productive conversation or look for a solution.

Emma and Mark's arguments only got worse throughout the months, resulting in a poisonous environment of hatred and bitterness in their house. Nothing appeared to help them get past their differences, even after they tried mediation, self-help books, and couples therapy. Their once-loving relationship turned into a war zone where neither of them was prepared to give in or make concessions in order to keep their marriage intact.

Emma and Mark's love became more and more obscured by hatred and animosity with every unsolved disagreement. They started to wonder if their differences prevented them from being genuinely compatible or if they were just too different. They eventually came to the painful conclusion that their relationship had failed, with each of them holding the other responsible.

Years later, Emma and Mark coincidentally crossed paths once more. They couldn't help but feel a twinge of grief for the love they had lost as they made small talk. They came to see that their failure to settle disputes constructively had been the main factor in their failure, and they regretted not having placed a higher priority on compromise and communication early on.

This narrative highlights the significance of excellent conflict resolution techniques in upholding a solid and long-lasting partnership by showing how unresolved disputes may weaken even the strongest of partnerships.

When conflict is effectively handled in a relationship

Sarah and Ryan were two strangers in the busy metropolis of Chicago who met by chance under the most unlikely of circumstances. Their first encounter occurred after a contentious debate about suggested modifications to their neighbourhood park during a community meeting. Sarah, an enthusiastic environmentalist, was vehemently against the growth plans, while Ryan, an astute architect, was in favour of advancement and creativity.

Sarah and Ryan had different opinions, but they were drawn to each other's enthusiasm and commitment. Instead of allowing their disagreements to separate them, they got into a passionate discussion and respectfully and empathetically exchanged thoughts and opinions. As the conference drew to an end, they realized that their mutual dedication to their community far exceeded their differences.

Sarah and Ryan kept running into one other at neighbourhood get-togethers and community events throughout the ensuing weeks. Every time, they found themselves having animated conversations about everything from art and culture to politics and urban planning. Even though they had different viewpoints, they were willing to listen to one another and kept an open mind throughout every discussion.

As their friendship grew, Sarah and Ryan realized that their differences presented chances for understanding and development rather than obstacles. They discovered how to resolve disputes amicably and humbly, reaching compromises and common ground in the face of difficulty. Their mutual regard, trust, and adoration were all nourished by their capacity to settle conflicts constructively.

Sarah and Ryan's relationship grew stronger as they collaborated to better their town; it went beyond friendship to become a deep, meaningful love. They came to see that the foundation of their partnership was a shared dedication to cooperation, compromise, and communication—values that would help them both overcome obstacles and celebrate victories in life.

Years later, in a lovely ceremony honouring their love and collaboration, Sarah and Ryan stepped in front of their friends and family to exchange vows. They realized as they gazed into each other's eyes that their relationship was proof of the effectiveness of conflict resolution, demonstrating that even the unlikeliest of alliances can succeed when they are based on mutual respect, understanding, and compromise.

This anecdote demonstrates how proficient dispute resolution techniques may both fortify a partnership and lay the groundwork for a robust and long-lasting bond.

Chapter Two

The Basic Questions

How can we settle disagreements in our marriage without endangering it?

Good communication, attentive listening, and a desire to reach a compromise are necessary for conflict resolution. When confronted with a conflict, listen to your spouse with empathy and respect, and concentrate on finding solutions rather than placing blame.

How can we keep disagreements from turning into ongoing problems in our marriage?

Address underlying issues, communicate honestly and openly about your needs and worries, and engage in active listening and empathy for your partner to avoid conflicts from turning into reoccurring problems. Rather than just settling the current situation, concentrate on coming up with compromises and solutions that deal with the underlying causes of conflicts.

How do we handle arguments or issues that come up often in our marriage?

Recurrent conflict resolution entails determining the root causes of the problem, having honest and open communication, and coming up with solutions that take into account the wants and worries of both parties. If you find yourself unable to settle disputes on your own, think about getting outside assistance.

How can we keep our marriage from experiencing recurrent arguments?

I am resolving underlying issues, drawing lessons from previous disputes, and altering communication or behaviour patterns that fuel conflict are all necessary to stop conflicts from happening again. As a relationship, strive to be flexible, adaptable, and eager to develop and learn.

How can we resolve disagreements in our marriage around domestic duties or chores?

Resolving disputes regarding domestic duties necessitates candid dialogue, flexibility, and a cooperative spirit. Fairly distribute the work, be transparent about expectations, and be adaptable in coming up with solutions that satisfy all parties.

How can we foster forgiveness in our marriage, and what part does forgiveness play in resolving conflicts?

Moving past disagreements and towards healing requires forgiveness. Develop empathy, let go of grudges, and live in the now rather than thinking about the past to help you forgive others. When necessary, apologize sincerely to your spouse, communicate honestly with them, and cooperate to mend the harm that disagreements have created.

In our marriage, how do we handle arguments that result from unsolved problems or traumatic experiences from the past?

Resolving disputes resulting from unresolved issues or prior traumas calls for both partners to be patient, kind, and supportive. Establish a secure environment for candid communication, acquire expert assistance if necessary, and cooperate to mend and move on as a pair.

How can we make sure that disagreements in our marriage are settled fairly and equally?

Establishing guidelines for polite conversation, placing a high value on empathy and active listening, and looking for win-win solutions are all necessary to ensure that disputes are settled fairly and equally. Steer clear of manipulation and power battles and collaborate as equal partners to create solutions that respect the interests and viewpoints of each party.

Following a disagreement or conflict, how can we reestablish connection and trust?

Establish open lines of communication, empathy, and understanding going ahead while admitting the adverse effects of the disagreement on the relationship and offering an apology if needed to reestablish trust and connection. Engage in active listening, empathy, and forgiveness, as well as emotional reconnection to fortify your relationship with your spouse.

How can we stop disagreements from turning into fights?

Refraining from escalating confrontations calls for the use of active listening techniques, maintaining composure, and taking breaks when feelings get intense. It's also critical to deal with problems as soon as possible rather than allowing them to worsen.

If our approaches to resolving conflicts disagree, how should we proceed?

It's critical to recognize and appreciate one another's conflict resolution strategies if you have diverse methods. Focus on shared objectives and ideals to reach a compromise and discover common ground.

How do we handle issues that keep coming up and never seem to be resolved?

Finding the underlying problems and patterns is necessary to resolve recurrent conflicts. Communicate your needs and concerns, engage in active listening, and collaborate to come up with original solutions.

Chapter Three

Some Untold Secrets to Conflict Resolution

How does forgiveness fit into a marriage's dispute resolution process?

Moving past disagreements and towards healing requires forgiveness. It entails apologizing, letting go of grudges, and pledging to work toward mending the relationship's connection and trust.

How can we undo the harm caused by cruel remarks or deeds committed during a dispute?

It takes honest regret, accepting responsibility for your acts, and expressing heartfelt apologies to undo the harm caused by harsh words or deeds. Try to mend the emotional connection and regain your partner's trust.

In a fight, what are some constructive ways to let out your anger?

Using "I" statements to communicate your feelings, pausing when your emotions get out of control, and engaging in assertive conversation without using blame or violence are all healthy methods to express anger.

How can we keep arguments from turning into a marriage-ending pattern?

Addressing underlying issues, honing good communication and conflict resolution techniques, and being proactive in seeking solutions rather than wallowing in old grievances are all necessary to stop conflicts from becoming recurrent cycles.

How can we stop disagreements from turning into heated debates?

Recognizing early indicators of tension, taking breaks to de-stress, and engaging in active listening and empathy exercises are all important in preventing disputes from getting worse.

How do we break free from a cycle of conflict that keeps coming up?

End the habit by recognizing the underlying problems and tendencies, being transparent and honest about your wants and feelings, and, if required, obtaining outside assistance. Be considerate and understanding of your partner's viewpoint, and collaborate to come up with ideas that both of you can agree on.

How can we stop disagreements from turning into furious debates?

Practice active listening, take breaks when emotions are running high, and use "I" words to communicate your wants and feelings without placing blame on your partner to stop disputes from getting worse. Instead of trying to win the dispute, concentrate on calming things down and finding common ground.

How can we foster forgiveness in our marriage, and what part does forgiveness play in resolving conflicts?

Rebuilding trust and a sense of connection in a relationship requires forgiveness in order to resolve past disagreements. By admitting your part in the disagreement, considering your partner's point of view, and making a commitment to let go of hurt and resentment, you can cultivate forgiveness. Be willing to forgive and move on as a couple, and show your partner empathy, compassion, and understanding.

How do we resolve disagreements when we think our spouse isn't paying attention to us or getting our point of view?

Seeking concessions that take into account both viewpoints, affirming each other's feelings, and using aggressive communication are all necessary for resolving arguments when one feels unheard.

How can we make sure that disagreements in our marriage don't cause further harm or hatred but rather foster growth and greater understanding?

Practising forgiveness and empathy, viewing disputes as teaching moments, and resolving conflicts in a way that fortifies relationships are all necessary to guarantee that conflicts result in progress.

How can we stop disagreements from turning into furious debates?

Remaining composed, engaging in active listening, and expressing your thoughts through "I" statements rather than placing blame or accusations on your spouse are all essential strategies for preventing arguments from getting out of hand. If necessary, take breaks and bring up the topic again when both parties are more relaxed.

How can we resolve a disagreement when we can't seem to agree?

Take a brief break to collect yourself and get perspective if you are unable to come to a decision. Schedule a time to review the discussion later when you're more relaxed, and if necessary, think about enlisting the assistance of a therapist or mediator.

How can we resolve disagreements in our marriage over money or financial matters?

Respect, compromise, and open communication are necessary for handling financial disputes. Together, create a budget, talk about your priorities and economic goals, and be prepared to make concessions in order to agree.

What typical blunders in communication can lead to more heated arguments in a marriage?

Blaming, criticizing, becoming defensive, and stonewalling are examples of typical communication errors. To stop arguments from getting worse, stay away from these actions and concentrate on problem-solving, active listening, and empathy.

What should we do if our techniques or styles for resolving conflicts differ?

If your approaches to handling disagreement differ, try to discover areas of agreement and respect each other's viewpoints. Develop your capacity for empathy, flexibility, and compromise to find solutions that benefit all parties.

How can we mend the harm that disagreements and fights have done to our marriage?

Repairing the harm caused by disagreements requires expressing genuine regret, accepting accountability for your deeds, and working to reestablish connection and trust with your spouse. Work on your empathy, patience, and forgiveness as you resolve the fallout from disagreements.

27

How can we foster an atmosphere that is conducive to settling disputes in our marriage?

Establishing guidelines for polite conversation, giving careful consideration to empathy and active listening, and making a firm commitment to resolving conflicts in a way that works for all parties are all part of creating a supportive environment. Schedule regular check-ins to handle problems as they come up and stop disputes from getting worse.

When there are arguments in a marriage, what are some constructive ways to let out outrage or frustration?

Using "I" words to communicate feelings, pausing if emotions go out of control, and engaging in active listening and empathy exercises are all healthy strategies to let out anger or irritation. Refrain from yelling, calling names, or using harsh language that could sour the connection.

Chapter Four

At The Place of Decision

How do we resolve disputes resulting from disparate priorities or values?

To resolve disputes resulting from different priorities or values, try to comprehend one another's viewpoints, look for areas of agreement, and consider making concessions that respect the needs and values of both parties. Engage in empathy and attentive listening, and go into the discussion with an open mind and a desire to come to a compromise.

What steps should we take if we can't settle a dispute amicably?

Seek outside assistance from a couple's therapist, counsellor, or mediator with expertise in this area. A qualified expert can offer direction, encourage fruitful dialogue, and assist couples in resolving disputes positively and healthily.

In a conflict, what are some constructive methods to let out irritation or anger?

Use "I" statements to communicate your wants and feelings, take breaks when needed to decompress, and communicate assertively rather than aggressively or defensively to manage your anger and frustration healthily. Respect and empathy for your partner should be maintained as you concentrate on solving the current problem.

What should we do if our preferences or styles for resolving conflicts differ?

It is possible for couples with disparate dispute resolution techniques to work together if they accept one another's methods, are willing to make concessions, and put the well-being of their relationship before being "right."

Resolving Conflict Caused by Critical Factors

How can we resolve disputes brought on by outside pressures or changes in our lives?

Put open communication, empathy, and support for one another's needs first while resolving disagreements brought on by outside stressors or life transitions. Work as a team to solve problems, discover solutions, and exercise patience and understanding.

What are some practical methods for resolving disputes before they get out of hand?

Using "I" words, accepting responsibility for your role in the conflict, and identifying common ground to work toward settlement are all effective de-escalation techniques.

How can we handle unresolved issues that keep coming up in our relationship?

Dealing with unsolved disputes calls for honest dialogue, comprehension of the underlying problems, and the discovery of workable solutions.

How can the hurt caused by arguments in our marriage be healed and trust restored?

Rebuilding trust entails owning up to previous wrongs, offering heartfelt apologies, and acting in a way that consistently meets your partner's needs and expectations.

How can we resolve disagreements over important life decisions like children or money without endangering our bond?

Active listening, open and honest communication, and a willingness to reach compromises that respect the needs and values of both parties are essential for resolving disputes involving significant choices.

How do we resolve disputes that have their roots in unfinished business or emotional baggage from the past?

Dealing with issues that have their roots in the past requires realizing how the past may be affecting present-day actions, getting help if necessary, and making a commitment to self-improvement and healing.

How can we keep disagreements from hurting our marriage in other ways, like intimacy or trust?

Dealing with disagreements as soon as they arise, being honest and transparent in your communication, and working to mend whatever harm they may have caused are all crucial ways to keep conflicts from influencing other aspects of your marriage. Make emotional closeness, trust, and connection a priority in your relationship, and even in the face of adversity, cooperate to build these areas.

In times of disagreement, how can we strike a balance between our own needs and wants and the demands of the relationship?

It takes empathy, compromise, and a readiness to put the health of the relationship first in order to strike a balance between each person's needs and wants and the needs of the partnership. Talk honestly with your partner about what you need, hear their side of the story, and look for solutions that will work for both of you and the relationship as a whole.

After arguments or confrontations, how can we mend our relationship and regain trust?

It takes time, work, and dedication from both parties to mend fences and fortify a relationship after a disagreement. Communicate honestly about your views and concerns, act with accountability, transparency, and consistency, and work to mend any harm your disagreements may have caused. In order to create a feeling of intimacy and connection in your relationship, give special attention to deeds of compassion, affection, and gratitude.

Chapter Five

Your Marriage and External Influences

How can we resolve financial disagreements in our marriage?

Handling financial disputes between spouses requires open communication, joint goal-setting, and budgeting that takes into account each partner's priorities and values. Seek agreements and be prepared to have frank conversations about money matters.

How can we resolve a disagreement over parenting choices?

Parenting decisions are a frequent topic of disagreement. Find compromises that put your kids' well-being first, listen to one other's viewpoints, and approach these conversations with compassion and understanding.

How should we resolve disputes with our in-laws or other relatives?

Managing disputes with in-laws or other family members necessitates establishing limits, being honest with your spouse about your worries, and, when required, putting up a united front. Prioritize your family's health and your marriage when coming up with answers.

What are some telltale signals that our marriage needs professional assistance or intervention to resolve conflicts?

Inability to resolve disagreements despite honest efforts, emotional or physical abuse, and ongoing conflicts that are negatively impacting the relationship are indicators that you may need professional treatment.

What should we do when we can't agree on anything crucial, like parenting or a career?

If you can't agree on anything significant, put mutual respect, open communication, and active listening first. When feasible, try to comprehend one another's points of view, consider opportunities for compromise, and work together to make decisions.

How can we resolve disputes in our marriage that result from divergent morals or ideologies?

Empathy, respect, and a desire to look for points of agreement are necessary when resolving conflicts resulting from disparities in values or views. Concentrate on appreciating one another's viewpoints, try to reach a compromise where you can, and decide to politely disagree on issues that are very important to each partner.

What are some significant signals that our marriage might benefit from outside assistance or counselling in order to overcome conflicts?

Difficult-to-resolve repeated problems, a breakdown in communication, or feelings of resentment or disconnection in the relationship are signs that you might benefit from outside support or counselling. Think about getting assistance from a therapist or counsellor who can offer direction, encouragement, and methods for resolving disputes constructively.

About the Author

ADEGBOYE S. ADURAGBEMI is a manager, business administrator, entrepreneur, and motivational speaker in Africa. ADEGBOYE has his BA from Yale University, IPMA from Adonai University, and a Masters in Business Administration (MBA) from the University of Salford, Manchester.

He was born in South Africa but is presently based in Nigeria as a motivational speaker and marriage counsellor in institutions, sectors, and seminars with young and upcoming managers all over Africa.

Acknowledgments

The credit for the practical completion of this medical report belongs to God. Without God's assistance, which has been a constant source of support and whose knowledge made this medical manuscript successful, it could have been impossible. My gratitude also goes out to my family, friends, well-wishers, and a countless number of other people who have supported me in various ways from the beginning of this text until its completion.